C000228238

Colourful Lent

A new way to pray when words are inadequate

Sheila Julian Merryweather

kevin mayhew

First published in 2005 by

KEVIN MAYHEW LTD
Buxhall, Stowmarket, Suffolk, IP14 3BW
E-mail: info@kevinmayhewltd.com
web: www.kevinmayhew.com

9 8 7 6 5 4 3 2 1 0

ISBN 1 84417 432 8
Catalogue No. 1500821

Cover design and typesetting by Angela Selfe

Printed and bound in Great Britain

Introduction

'He was in the wilderness 40 days.'
Mark 1:13

Lent is upon us. Don't we all have rather mixed feelings about this season? For some there is a sense of expectancy – Easter must be on the way. For some there is a sense of apprehension. So often in the past it has been a time of strict discipline and harsh measures, full of recommendations to give up those things of which we are fond and take upon ourselves those things which are burdensome.

This Lent, I would like to dare to be with Jesus in the wilderness. I hope that you will come with me. It's not a place where any of us normally choose to be and yet at several times during our lives we find ourselves there. We experience the wilderness. It is a hard, lonely place, but we forget that it can be turned to good effect and that the angels will minister to us. Jesus has been there before us and so he does understand.

As we think about going into the wilderness I wonder whether you, like me, experience a resistance. Before we set forth, therefore, it's as well to pray and try to sort out what is causing the unwillingness even to start.

I find that if I use colour as I pray, I can express what I feel about a situation in a more realistic way than words can do.

The circle of colour that you see below was the result of my praying about the beginning of Lent and entering the wilderness.

I used the colours as I was considering what was stopping me from making a start.

 This represents the feeling of not knowing, of feeling lost, through which other senses gradually emerge.

 This represents my fear of what may lie ahead.

 This represents the paralysis that overtakes me when considering difficult topics. I can so easily get stuck.

 This is the anxiety which tends to take over.

 The green shows my belief that if I do step forward into Lent, into the wilderness in a positive spirit, then growth will take place.

 This is just there. It's my belief that God is in the wilderness too. Jesus was led there by the Spirit and so are we.

Suggestion

As I have shared my prayer circle with you, why not try to use colour as you pray about Lent and what it means to you.

If you have not used colour in this way before, you might find it helpful to start with a small circle. Circles are always complete, however large or small.

As you pray about entering the wilderness of Lent with Jesus, just use any colours that come into your mind. Don't analyse what you are doing. Let your prayer and the colour flow.

Later, when you look back at your circle, you'll find that it can help you in different ways.

1

'The angels ministered to him.'
Mark 1:13

We can enter the wilderness for the wrong reasons. It can be an attempt at escapism.

At one time, I was looking after a school in the middle of Sabah, Malaysia. We were five days up-river, so I could go nowhere except into the jungle which surrounded us. Even the children knew that was forbidden unless one went with several others because of the dangers lurking there.

I was angry and frustrated and felt I'd got to get away from people – large and small – and so I strode off into the jungle on my own. I thought I only needed to keep near to the river on my right to find my way back. I thought I could sort out my difficulties if I could just be alone, and there was nowhere else for that to happen.

I had, as it were, chosen my own wilderness to be in, but it was not God's time or place. God knew as I did, deep down, that I needed to confront and talk with the other people concerned, not to run away.

My way of coping with anger had always been to go off for long walks, or rather 'strides', until I felt better. That, however, did not work this time. I couldn't stride in the jungle. I had to walk very carefully if I were to avoid falling over tree roots or stepping on a snake, or getting caught up in the liana hanging down at head level. I lost sight of the river very quickly, but I could hear it and so plodded on.

After a while, I suddenly realised I could no longer hear the river. I was lost. When I tried to retrace my steps, all paths – such as they were – looked alike. The trees were so dense and tall that I could no longer see the sky. I sat on a tree root and gave way to despair.

I had forgotten that God would send his angels! Even if I'd remembered, I wouldn't have believed that they were for me. It was my own fault that I had ended up where I was, lost.

However, the angels came – in the form of two small 8-year-old boys. They had seen me heading off into the jungle and had had no time to tell anyone else, so they followed me themselves.

They had sensed that I needed to be on my own and so had kept their distance and didn't show themselves until they knew that I was completely lost. They, of course, were at home in the jungle and so came up to me, and each taking one of my hands led me to safety.

I learned a lot from that self-chosen wilderness experience. The wilderness is a dangerous place. We may find ourselves there, led by the Spirit. Then we can enter trustfully, as did Jesus after his baptism. He needed the space and time to consider his future ministry. He needed to be alone with his God.

When we look back over our wilderness experiences, we see that they can be of a few hours' duration or can last for days or months. Some people feel most of their lives have been spent in the wilderness as they've had little awareness of God's presence with them. As happened to Jesus, some people are made more aware of their 'demons' than of God at such times.

I can look back and pray about such experiences in colour. I know that I am not aware of God most of the time but that he most certainly has been with me and has led me to this day.

Suggestion

Take time this week to look back over your life and see if in retrospect you can recognise the times when God's Spirit was leading and supporting you.

You could do this in many ways. You might like to do a circle for each period of your life, as above, or you might look back at significant events and see where God was at those times.

At the time, I did not necessarily see the yellow and orange as showing that God was, as it were, trying to make himself heard, but I know now that he's been there all the way.

Of course, God is in all colours and all life, but using colours in this symbolic way with prayer can strengthen our faith.

2

'The Spirit immediately drove him out into the wilderness.'
Mark 1:12

This translation brought me up short. There's all the difference in the world between being led and being driven. Whichever way it was for Jesus, he did the Spirit's bidding.

I think most of us tend to feel we're driven by circumstances rather than led by the Spirit where there's more of an element of free choice. We can choose to follow or not, but if we're driven we feel we have no freedom. Maybe that's why I always want to rebel on Ash Wednesday!

In 1 Kings 19:9-10, Elijah must have felt driven by God. Even when he had had enough and had hidden away in a cave because, as he said, 'I, only I, am left', God found him and asked, 'What are you doing here, Elijah?' God had yet more in store for him.

Poor Elijah, he did have a tough time, mostly driven by God. Read his story in 1 Kings if you're not familiar with it.

I believe God does sometimes have to drive us, to propel us to take certain steps. But then we have the freedom either to go forward or to take a different path.

For some it can feel like the wilderness when they enter a religious community. Everything is so strange and unknown. We hear people say, 'God had to push me here, I'd never have come of my own volition. It's crazy to give up my independence and all that life has given me.' However, when we persevere and find our attitudes being turned upside down, we realise we are happily following God's call and no longer being driven by it. We have stopped fighting and have entered into the life fully. We become more truly ourselves.

I believe that Jesus was driven rather than led by the Spirit into the wilderness. He knew that for him the future could be an ordeal and that he would be reluctant to face the decisions he would have to make regarding his ministry. He had to face up to the fact that he could easily use his power to gain popularity and become a highly successful leader. He had to decide what sort of leader his Father wanted him to be. Surely he was tempted to return home and lead a quiet life as a carpenter? He could still pray that God's kingdom would come.

He could only sort out his future by making time and space in which to pray through all the options before him.

Suggestion

Could we this week consider prayerfully where we are in relation to God? Are we being nudged by God's Spirit and ignoring him? Are we being driven and fighting against it? Are we being driven and rather reluctantly going along?

Let us enter the quiet space and ask God's Spirit to show us the way. Wherever, however I am, God is waiting to help me along.

Perhaps I'm stuck.   Perhaps I'm just blank.

 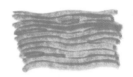

Perhaps I'm confused.   Perhaps I'm peaceful.

Can you use colour to pray how you are with God? It can sometimes help to make things clearer for us.

God understands our colours. Obviously your choice of colours and expression will be different from mine.

3

'He was tempted.'
Mark 1:13

At different stages of our lives we all have to make serious decisions. These decisions usually affect others as well as ourselves and are therefore never straightforward.

For example, parents have to decide how their children are to be educated, or someone wins or inherits a great deal of money. Are they going to change their lifestyles as a result? These are very different but difficult decisions.

Each one of us has to decide what we are going to do with our lives. That's an ongoing decision as our paths through life twist and turn. We cannot see into the future. I'm not sure I'd want to! It would be too overwhelming.

Little did I know when I wanted to be a teacher that I'd find myself teaching in the jungle in Borneo and on a desert island in the Solomon Islands. We can only see a small step at a time, and each step has to be taken carefully, prayerfully, with all the help we can find.

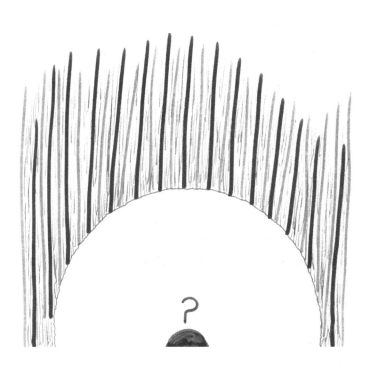

When we have an important decision to make, we can feel very alone. Others do not seem to understand our difficulties. They sometimes impute wrong motives to us.

God can use our 'wrong motives', though. I'm sure it was a reaction to the loneliness of years that drove me into Community. However, it was a motive that God could use to take me where he wanted me to be.

At such times we are really in a wilderness place, just as we see Jesus being at the beginning of his ministry.

When I pray for discernment, I see myself in a place like this.

I can see no way forward and am overtaken by anxiety. I can see no one who can help. I cannot see ahead. It's as though there's a dark fog or mist surrounding me. At such a time I can only be patient. I must wait and pray, wait and pray . . .

As time goes by, I begin to identify the choices before me. It's not usually an either/or choice but one of many. Although I begin to see different paths I could follow, I still cannot see ahead. I still need to go on being patient, waiting upon God in prayer. Jesus took 40 days to find his answers, so we needn't be surprised that we take much longer.

We forget sometimes that God does give us help in hard decision-making. Helpful writers and speakers can give us new insights. Wise friends are sometimes on hand. These may disagree with each other, but we have ears to hear. We know when what is being said is true for us. We know God has been with us in our past experience. He's not going to leave us now.

Even if we make a wrong or unwise decision, God stays with us and will help us through. 'All things work together for good with those who love him' (*Romans 8:28*).

As we pray, we begin to see that God is beckoning us on. He is in the mist that blocks our view.

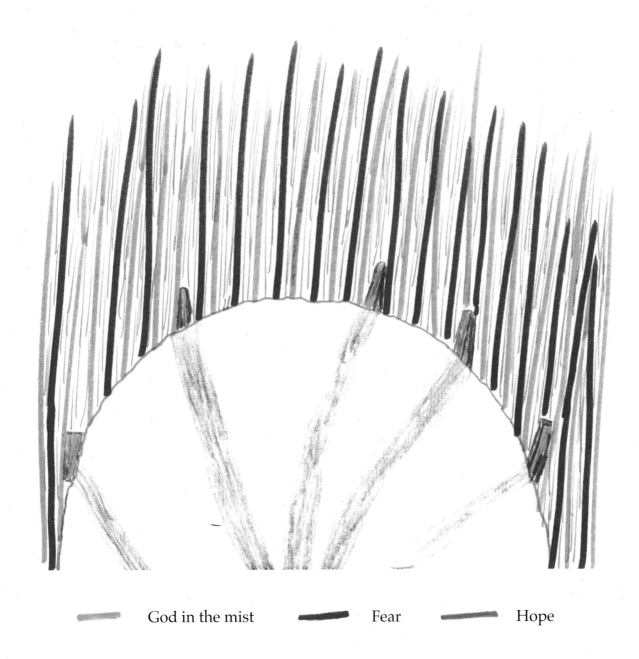

—— God in the mist　　—— Fear　　—— Hope

As we come closer to making a decision, the fear and apprehension grow. The nearer we come, though, an element of hope also creeps in. The hope helps us to take the next step: God is there before us. As Julian of Norwich says, 'All shall be well and all manner of things shall be well.'

How difficult it must have been for Jesus as he tried to face the future during his time in the wilderness. Should he use his power to convince people that he was the

Son of God? Should he take on the mantle of the Suffering Servant? Was opting out altogether an option for him? Surely he considered it.

His faith in his Father was certainly put to the test during those 40 days of what must have been mental distress and torment. He knew, too, what it would cost his mother Mary and later his friends Mary, Martha and Lazarus – all his disciples and followers. However, did he manage to convince himself that the way of the cross was the only way for him?

Suggestion

During this week, can we try to look at the decisions we have made or that we face, and see if we are really on God's side, as he is on ours?

4

'You shall worship the Lord your God.'
Matthew 4:10

The creeds and the constant theological arguments of the Church can be a real stumbling-block at times. It's as though everything we have ever believed is gradually, or suddenly, taken from under us. We are left with nothing to hang on to, amidst all the discordant voices.

Life's experiences can do the same thing. I had always believed that if I carried out God's will for me to the best of my ability, then God would look after me and keep me safe.

However, that was not the case. At various times during my years in Malaysia and the Solomons I was physically attacked, rocks were thrown at me, I had all my possessions taken from me, and was very ill. Could I still believe in a personal, caring God?

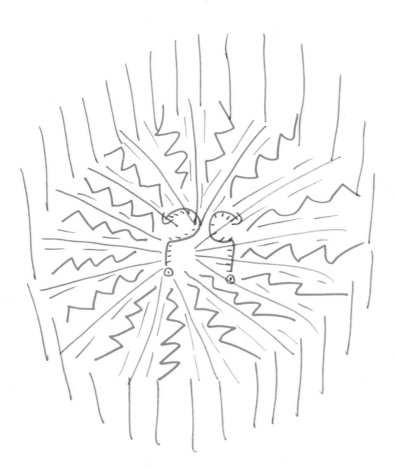

At such times, we are once again in the wilderness. How did Jesus come to terms with what lay ahead of him? We cannot know.

Each of us has wilderness experiences. The wilderness is a silent place. We leave behind all those discordant voices. They are of no help. We are empty.

We search for God with nothing in our hands, as did Jesus. We no longer try to argue or persuade ourselves that we believe this theory or that. We are lost . . .

We are lost – and we are found.

God can get through to us when we stop struggling. We can hear when we truly listen. We discover that we do have faith in God and God has faith in us. It is hidden deep down underneath all the arguments and turmoil of trying to understand.

It is in the wilderness that we can be still.

'Be still and know that I am God.'
Psalm 46:10

We can go forth again from the wilderness knowing that the foundation stone of our faith is strong enough to hold us through all the changing expressions of the Church's beliefs that sway around us. We can join in once more, trying to understand and express our faith without losing the pearl of great price. Ultimately, it is our faith that holds us. Beliefs change; faith holds on.

Security

Beliefs?
Creeds?
Convictions?
Standards?
Certainty?

No.

No more certainty.
No more footholds.
No more handholds.
Nothing is stable or sure.
Nothing to hold on to any more.

Only the conviction that I am held.

I often think of the group of 10 Taiwanese sailors who turned up one Sunday morning at church in Sandakan-Sabah. They all came to the family Eucharist which that day was in English. They did not 'understand' one word of it, but they gave themselves completely to the mystery and wonder of the worship. They touched base, as it were, with their God and returned to sea upheld, knowing God was with them.

I think their experience was similar to one of mine many years earlier. By chance (?), I found myself attending the service of Benediction. I had no idea at that time of what it was all about, but the whole atmosphere of worship and transcendence caught me. I think I found God that night – or God found me.

Suggestion

Would you like to think back to a similar experience that you have had? A time when you knew God's love was with you in a very real way.

Pray and give thanks and if you can, express in colour how you felt at the time. To remember and relive such experiences can help to hold us through wilderness times.

5

'He was with the wild beasts.'
Mark 1:13

The wilderness is certainly a dangerous place.

On the first day of working on this section, I could get nowhere. I sat with my pen and paper, surrounded by colours, and produced nothing. I was feeling fairly desperate by the time I gave up and went to bed.

Next morning I woke up after a very powerful dream. Dreams are meant to be taken seriously, especially those that come to us during wilderness times.

In this dream I was in a wilderness. It was a large area of what appeared to be grass, but wasn't. It was more like green baize. I had a vacuum cleaner with me, and was trying to pick up all the bits.

I saw one small pile of dirt which I thought I should tackle. The whole area would look really attractive if I just cleared that away. I took my hoover and started to collect it up. Then the whole pile exploded! It was horrific! What looked like giant cockroaches rushed in all directions, soon covering the area I had been cleaning. There was also a myriad of ant-like insects. I fought them with my hoover but there were far too many. I was frantic.

Then a very large, black crow-like bird flew down. I thought it was going to attack me, but no, it was a friend. It started eating the ants and cockroaches and had the feast of its life.

I seized the opportunity and tried to leave the area, but it wasn't to be, not yet. I left the green place and tried to climb up some rocks but these proved false, just as the grass had been. I sank up to my waist in mud instead. I couldn't move. Terrified, I woke up.

Now that I look back at that dream, it tells or reminds me of so many truths regarding the experience of being in the wilderness. When we have what we believe to be a significant dream, it is helpful to write it down. But don't leave it there. Think about it, pray about it.

I find it helpful to use colour as I think and pray. The colours often reveal more of the dream than I can explain in words. This is how I experienced that dream.

Usually a growth colour but this green is not deep. Not real growth.

 Afraid

 and angry – trying to fight back.

 Under attack.

 Powerful and small but insistent.

 Unknown power. 'Angel in disguise?' or demon.

 Anxiety.

Dreams don't have all the answers. They can leave us with as many questions as answers, but they are usually questions that we haven't considered before.

The big question that this dream left with me is how to approach a wilderness. How to approach a season like Lent, or a retreat.

I went in with a vacuum cleaner! I was evidently keen to get my house in order. I was going to use the time to tackle anything that showed up in the way of sin or ugliness. I wanted my life to look good.

I wonder how many of you this Lent are still hoovering away? We may be in danger of disturbing a hornets' nest. Is that what God wants us to do? Are we so busy looking at ourselves and all that is wrong with our lives that we cease to see God? I'm not sure.

We are called to repent, but I have a strong suspicion that the best way of repenting is to focus on God, not on ourselves. If we spend too much time 'vacuuming' we are in danger of losing sight of God. We cease to hear his voice. The clamour of all that comes at us drowns out the Holy Spirit.

At some level, we need to accept the wilderness as it is. As in the well-known hymn by G. H. Smyttan and F. Pott, 'Forty days and forty nights', the wild beasts prowl around but we don't have to tackle them all and not on our own. We're not fighting some battle to improve ourselves. We're trying to follow our Lord's lead, to hear his voice.

In the dream I was certainly very busy trying to improve my wilderness. But I only succeeded in making it far worse. It may have been better if I had been able to ignore the cockroaches and ants. If I had just sat still and let God – the crow? – take over then I might not have ended up in the mud!

Here is a poem I wrote after an earlier, similar experience.

Clear water

I cease to stir the well.
Let the water settle.
The mud has had its day.
It clouded what was there.
I saw only dirt and filth.
No life – no movement.

Now the sun shines through.
The water sparkles.
Lights flash through
too fast to grasp.
But moments of new life and hope appear.

Another question the dream left me holding is with regard to angels. The crow really scared me at first, but it proved to be an ally. Do we give people whom we find difficult or scary time to prove themselves to be angels? People God has deliberately put in our paths to help us in some way. It is so easy to avoid those whom we find less attractive, as I fled from the crow. When we do flee, we could be rejecting God's help.

One more question I am faced with is about the basic falsity of the green in this dream. It is a colour of growth, but there was no grass. The rocks were false, too. It's as though I was trying to make a wilderness that I could manage, a comfortable place where I could sort out problems and not be too disturbed while I did it.

Don't we all try to do that in Lent? We make a Lenten rule for ourselves that we think we can manage. We sometimes select a Lenten course or special Lenten services which we think would be rather good to attend. Of course, these can be very helpful options for us, ones that we need to take, but my dream has left me wondering whether perhaps one Lent it would be better to come to grips with what comes my way each day, keeping my eyes and ears open for God and his angels.

If you do dream dreams, hang on to them. As you go on looking at them, you will find them speaking to you more and more. No one can interpret your dream for you. It is yours alone. Keep it safe.

Suggestion

Can you remember any of your dreams? If you can, try praying with one of them and use colour as you do so. Perhaps you can spread the dream over a large sheet of paper. It helps not to have boundaries when working on a dream.

If you return to your colour-prayed dream a few days later, you'll see more in it than you did at the time. God can – and does – reach us through our dreams.

6

'They led him away to crucify him.'
Matthew 27:31

An enormous number of people are suffering today as did Jesus and – dare I say it? – more than he did. Today some we know suffer torture, both physical and mental, for years; some in isolation with no understanding of why, or knowledge of how long they are to remain incarcerated.

Let us not forget Mary, either. How she suffered, seeing her son being rejected and so brutally treated, and knowing her own helplessness. There was nothing she could do. How many mothers and fathers are in the same situation today! So many suffer for years, not knowing what has become of lost children. Have they been abused, turned into child soldiers, slaves or sexual toys . . . ? They do not even know if their children are still alive. Which is worse, knowing or not knowing? Both result in immeasurable agony of mind and spirit.

As for us who have not had to experience such pain, we can only attempt to hang on to the belief that Jesus is there in the midst of today's suffering as he was on the cross. The truth of the incarnation – God with us – makes little sense if that ended on the cross. How else can we respond to all the cries for help from the victims of natural disasters, such as the tsunami of 2004 in south and south-east Asia? We can at least understand man-made catastrophies, such as the fall of the twin towers in New York in 2001. But earthquakes, cyclones, floods or drought? There are no answers to these.

Even Jesus on the cross could understand why he had ended up there. It was the only outcome of following his integrity. When we talk of keeping our integrity, aren't we saying that we can only keep following what we believe to be God's will for us? We deny that inner voice we believe comes from the Spirit of God when we betray our own integrity.

We know that Holy Week culminates in Easter. Yet we struggle to hang on to that belief in the midst of horror or disaster. How much harder for those who do not have that faith in the Resurrection. Pray for them and for ourselves, that we will maintain our faith when we find ourselves in the wilderness of suffering.

You may find it helpful to use colour as you pray at such times.

In the depth of suffering, one can feel very alone, boxed in by the hurt and helplessness of the situation. Is this how Jesus felt when he cried out, 'My God, my God, why have you forsaken me?'

How hard is it to add a colour which symbolises for you God's presence and support and understanding of us in the suffering? Try to do this.

If you find it difficult to do, pray in the words of the distraught father, 'Lord, I believe. Help my unbelief.'

Looking at this prayer square now, we can see that God is truly with us in our suffering today. He hurts when we hurt. Otherwise, God would be less caring than we are, and that cannot be true. Jesus' whole life spoke of love and compassion for others.

As God still hurts in the hurt and suffering of his people, so he rejoices in the overflowing and selflessness of so many.

At the end of Lent, hopefully we can leave the wilderness, but we all know we shall find ourselves there again one day. However, we leave in a stronger position than we were on Ash Wednesday.

Our Lord found himself ministered to by angels. We too will be helped by them, just as the two small boys rescued me from the jungle. We know from the Gospels that Jesus didn't cease to be tempted. The Devil left him for a season. May we be on the alert and ready to recognise our own 'demons' when they reappear, as surely they will.

However, whatever language we use, we have the sure knowledge of faith, the assurance of God with us through our joys, and our sorrows, our lack of love. We know that God does not give up on us.

Jesus could have avoided the cross if he had played a political hand – if he had not kept his integrity. He couldn't, though, *not* do as his Father wished, and so he suffered. So many have followed in his footsteps. Charles de Foucauld, for one, refused to give up his life of witness. Some of you may find his prayer helpful.

Prayer of Abandonment

Father, I abandon myself into your hands;
do with me what you will.
Whatever you may do, I thank you;
I am ready for all, I accept all.
Let only your will be done in me and in all your
creatures. I wish no more than this, O Lord.
Into your hands I commend my soul.
I offer it to you with all the love of my heart, for I
love you, Lord, and so need to give myself, to
surrender myself into your hands without
reserve and with boundless confidence, for you
are my Father.

Charles de Foucauld (1858-1916)

Holy Week reminds us so much of our Lord's outpouring of love. Not only in his death on the cross on Good Friday, but in his love shown in the hours just before, as he gave all he could in the way of continuing support by giving himself in the bread and wine at the Last Supper. He knew what was to follow, but his last hours were spent living to the full for his friends and followers – and for us.

He gives himself today. He wants his people to be at one with him and one another. How dare we make the sacrament of Holy Communion the cause of division with our different interpretations, explanations and meanings?

It was Queen Elizabeth I who said,

> 'Twas God the word that spake it,
> he took the bread and brake it;
> and what the word did make it;
> that I believe, and take it.

The Eucharist is a mystery and we shall all be united with our Lord and each other if we let go of our wranglings. I have long since stopped thinking about what the Sacrament 'means'. I just know that in receiving the bread and the wine, we belong to God and to each other. We are all 'enfolded in love', as Julian of Norwich said. That is enough for me.

We know in our hearts that God needs each one of us to express his love for his world and people. As St Theresa of Avila said, 'He has no hands but our hands.' That message comes through loud and clear in our Lord's washing of the disciples' feet during those crucial last few hours.

I sometimes find Holy Saturday the most difficult day of Holy Week. It throws me back to Ash Wednesday. The wilderness is all around me once more – emptiness and loneliness.

Yet we cannot enter the experience of Mary and the disciples completely because we know that our Lord triumphed and triumphs still in lives lived for, and in him. We rejoice in the knowledge that as a result of the Resurrection of Christ, God is still with us and always shall be, through all our wilderness experiences, through all our lives.

'Lo, I am with you always, to the close of the age' (*Matthew 28:20*).

Alleluia!

God is hurt by all the suffering that comes to his people. He receives this suffering on the cross and transforms it, new life rising from it.

As we approach God at the centre, through joy or depression, through strife or peace, we become closer to each other and to God.

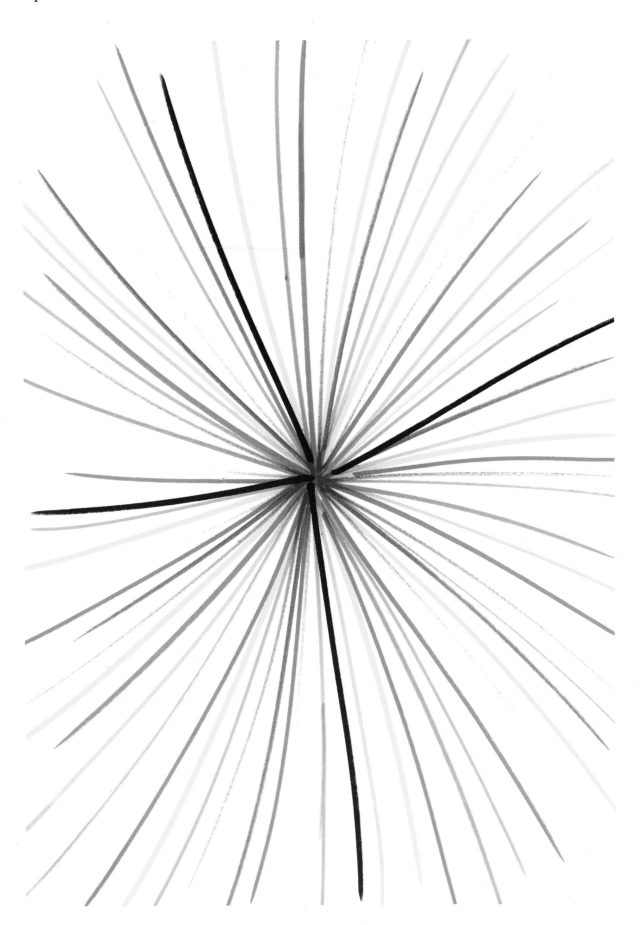

Also available
by Sheila Julian Merryweather

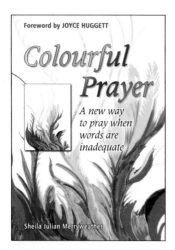

Colourful Prayer
ISBN 1 84417 049 7
Order No. 1500575

At the heart of Sheila Julian Merryweather's highly successful and innovative *Colourful Prayer* is the concept that colour is often more helpful than words and therefore a valuable prayer tool. Colour-prayers are spontaneous 'doodles' using only felt-tip pens.

An outline plan for a day's workshop is included for those who wish to discover colour-prayers in more detail.

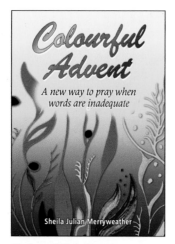

Colourful Advent
ISBN 1 84417 273 2
Order No. 1500710

Sheila Julian Merryweather shares her personal experience of using colour to pray about some of the difficult traditional themes of Advent – death, judgement, hell – and, in doing so, encourages and inspires the reader to use colour in a similar way.

This unique approach to Advent will be welcomed by those who struggle to pray with just words or those who seek to add a whole new dimension to their prayer life.